MW00780872

Inspirational Quips and Quotes for Living the Christian Life

By

Dr. E. K. Bailey

Compiled by
Jeaninne Stokes

☙

© 2015 by Jeaninne Stokes

To the best of the compiler's knowledge
and research, all quotes are original of the
author.

Scripture taken from the Holy Bible, New
International Version®
Copyright © 1973, 1978, 1984
Biblica used by permission.
All rights reserved worldwide.

Bio & Cover Picture: Courtesy of
Moody Publishers

Back cover picture: Courtesy of
Paul Ransom Photography

Editing services: Provided by
Marilyn Bradford

Published by: JStokes Publishing
Arlington, TX 76018
www.jstokeswritingministries.com

ISBN: 978-0692602300

All rights reserved. No part of this
publication may be reproduced or
transmitted for commercial purposes,
except for brief quotations in printed
reviews, without written permission
of the publisher.
Printed in the United States of America

BAILEYISM

**A memorable saying
shared by
Dr. E. K. Bailey during
his Pastoral years to
challenge and inspire
people to live the
Christian life
effectively.**

This book is dedicated
to the legacy of
Dr. E. K. Bailey

CONTENTS

Baileyisms on ...

A well-read soul is a well-fed soul.

When your words came, I ate them; they were my joy and my heart's delight.

Jeremiah 15:16

Baileyism #2

Don't run thru the Bible too fast because you may run over something important.

Open my eyes that I may see wonderful things in your law.

Psalms 119:18

Always come to church with a pen in one hand and your Bible in the other.

Do your best to present yourself to God as one approved.

II Timothy 2:15

BAILEYISM #4

Bring your Bible to church; it is your sword and weapon of defense.

Take the sword of the Spirit, which is the word of God.

Ephesians 6:17

BAILEYISM #5

Bring a long pen to church for your short memory.

Open my eyes that I may see wonderful things in your law.

Psalms 119:18

BAILEYISM #6

A church is for sinners like a hospital is for sick people.

Come to me, all you who are weary and burdened, and I will give you rest.

Matthew 11:28

Church Attendance

BAILEYISM #7

Christians come to church every Sunday to determine the play they will use to beat their opponent - the devil.

Put on the full armor of God so that you can take your stand against the devil's schemes.

Ephesians 6:11

BAILEYISM #8

**You miss a blessing if
you leave church
before the
benediction is given.**

*May the LORD, the
maker of heaven and
earth, bless you from
Zion.*

Psalms 134:3

Church Attendance

BAILEYISM #9

When the president walks in church, everyone should stand up, but when Jesus walks in, everyone should fall down.

Ascribe to the Lord the glory due his name. Worship the LORD in the splendor of his holiness.

Psalms 29:2

BAILEYISM #10

**Stop looking for the
perfect church, for
when you join, it will
become imperfect.**

*There is no one righteous,
not even one.*

Romans 3:10

Church Attendance

BAILEYISM #11

If you don't praise God in public, you won't praise him in private.

I will bless the LORD at all times. His praise will always be on my lips.

Psalms 34:1

Church Attendance

BAILEYISM #12

A church is designed to be a red sea, not a dead sea.

I know your deeds. You have a reputation of being alive, but you are dead.

Revelation 3:1

BAILEYISM #13

If you come to church to do anything other than to worship, your coming is in vain.

I will bless the Lord at all time; his praise shall continually be in my mouth.

Psalms 34:1

Church Growth

You can't lead people from behind.

I urge you to live a life worthy of the calling you have received.

Ephesians 4:1

Church leaders should model growth, not perfection.

Set an example for the believers in speech, in life, in love, in faith and in purity.

I Timothy 4:12

BAILEYISM #16

If you use all of your bullets shooting rabbits, you won't have any left when the bears come.

Avoid foolish controversies and genealogies and arguments and quarrels about the law, because these are unprofitable and useless.

Titus 3:9

Church Leadership

BAILEYISM #17

If you aim for zero, you will hit it every time.

Work hard so you can present yourself to God and receive his approval.

2 Timothy 2:15

BAILEYISM #18

Every leader should surround themselves with a few good men.

Brothers, choose seven men from among you who are known to be full of the Spirit and wisdom.

Acts 6:3

Church Leadership

BAILEYISM #19

The church is not your church; it's God's church.

When the Chief Shepherd appears, you will receive the crown of glory that will never fade away.

I Peter 5:4

Never be afraid to face what's facing you.

So do not fear for I am with you; do not be dismayed, for I am your God.

Isaiah 41:10

BAILEYISM #21

Just because you're saved, doesn't mean you're a sissy.

The Lord is my light and my salvation, so why should I be afraid?

Psalms 27:1

If you're not sure who to vote for, vote your convictions.

Whatever is true, honorable, right, pure, and lovely and of good repute, if there is any excellence and if anything worthy of praise, dwell on these things.

Philippians 4:8

BAILEYISM #23

You are who you are when no one is watching.

To the pure you show yourself pure, but to the wicked you show yourself hostile.

Psalms 18:26

Courage

BAILEYISM #24

Fish don't swim in
shallow water; if you
want to catch fish,
you'll need to launch
into the deep.

*Go therefore and make
disciples of all nations.*

Matthew 28:19

Evangelism

BAILEYISM #25

Don't be so heavenly minded that you are of no earthly good.

The harvest is plentiful but the workers are few.

Luke 10:2

BAILEYISM #26

If Jesus tells you a mouse can pull a house, don't ask any questions - just hitch it up.

Everything is possible for him who believes.

Mark 9:23

Faith

BAILEYISM #27

Faith is acting like something is so, even when it is not so, so that it will be so.

Faith is being sure of what we hope for and certain of what we do not see.

Hebrews 11:1

BAILEYISM #28

The will of God can always be found in the word of God.

Your word is a lamp for my feet and a light for my path.

Psalms 119:105

BAILEYISM #29

If you are not obeying what God has already revealed to you, there is no way you will know what he wants to reveal to you.

To those who are open to my teaching, more understanding will be given.

Mark 4:25

BAILEYISM #30

Everything that happens to a believer is either God sent or God allowed.

You would have no power over me unless it was given to you from above.

John 19:11

BAILEYISM #31

If you are your greatest cause, you have a mighty little cause.

God opposes the proud but gives grace to the humble.

James 4:6

BAILEYISM #32

Sometimes you have to get smaller before you can get bigger.

Whoever exalts himself will be humbled, and whoever humbles himself will be exalted.

Matthew 23:12

BAILEYISM #33

God can use a person with an educated head and a consecrated heart.

I have hidden your word in my heart that I might not sin against you.

Psalms 119:11

BAILEYISM #34

A Ph.D. without G–O-D is just an educated devil.

Don't be impressed with your own wisdom. Instead, fear the Lord and turn your back on evil.

Proverbs 3:7

BAILEYISM #35

It's okay to have your name written down in many books, but it's better to have your name written down in one book - the Book of Life.

If anyone's name was not found written in the book of life, he was thrown into the lake of fire.

Revelation 20:15

BAILEYISM #36

The measure of a man is not how great he is in his faith, but how great he is in his love.

By this all men will know that you are my disciples, if you love one another.

John 13:35

BAILEYISM #37

Theology without love is like a lamp without a light; a body without life; a car without gasoline.

If I had the gift of prophecy, and if I knew all the mysteries of the future, but did not love others, what good would I be?

I Corinthians 13:2

BAILEYISM #38

**Before you say
something about
anyone else,
ask yourself:
"Is it kind? Is it true?
Is it necessary?"**

*Let everything you say be
good and helpful, so that
your words will be an
encouragement to those
who hear them.*

Ephesians 4:29

Loving Others

BAILEYISM #39

**If you really want
your life to count,
invest in people,
because when you are
gone, your life will
still bear fruit.**

*When you produce much
fruit, you are my true
disciples.*

John 15:8

Loving Others

BAILEYISM #40

Your spouse is like sandpaper-God uses them to smooth out your rough edges.

It is not good for the man to be alone. I will make a helper suitable for him.

Genesis 2:18

Marriage

BAILEYISM #41

The best thing a father can do for a child is to love his mother.

Husbands ought to love their wives as their own bodies. He who loves his wife loves himself.

Ephesians 5:28

Marriage

BAILEYISM #42

The husband is the band that holds the house together.

Husbands love your wives, just as Christ loved the church and gave himself up for her.

Ephesians 5:25

Marriage

BAILEYISM #43

**Children don't want
to hear you preach
with your mouth, but
with your life.**

*Be an example to all
believers in what you
teach, in the way you live,
in your love, your faith
and your purity.*

I Timothy 4:12

Parenting

BAILEYISM #44

Discipline without loving instruction produces rebellion.

Fathers, do not exasperate your children; instead, bring them up in the training and instruction of the Lord.

Ephesians 6:4

Parenting

BAILEYISM #45

**Never are you more
than a man than
when you are tender
with your children.**

*Let your gentleness be
evident to all.
The Lord is near.*

Philippians 4:5

BAILEYISM #46

We cannot isolate our children from the world, but we can insulate them from the world.

Start children off on the way they should go, and even when they are old they will not turn from it.

Proverbs 22:6

BAILEYISM #47

A tent prayer is a prayer that covers a whole lot of stuff but touches nothing.

When you pray, do not keep on babbling like pagans, for they think they will be heard because of their many words.

Matthew 6:7

Prayer

BAILEYISM #48

Why should God answer your prayers when all you're going to do is help yourself?

The Lord is far from the wicked, but he hears the prayer of the righteous.

Proverbs 15:29

Baileyism #49

**Don't let your
problems get you
down -
except on your knees.**

*Let us approach the
throne of grace with
confidence, so that we
may receive mercy and
find grace to help us in
our time of need.*

Hebrews 4:16

Prayer

BAILEYISM #50

Prayer gives you a full tank when your courage and strength are running on empty.

*As soon as I pray, you answer me;
you encourage me by giving me strength.*

Psalms 138:3

BAILEYISM #51

Be ye always ready, for if you are not, it will be a long time before you preach again.

Preach the Word and be prepared, whether the time is favorable or not.

II Timothy 4:2

BAILEYISM #52

Preachers, always give the Lord a prepared mind and a rested body.

Preach the Word and be prepared, whether the time is favorable or not.

II Timothy 4:2

The hour of examination is not the hour of preparation.

Be a good worker, one who does not need to be ashamed and who correctly explains the word of truth.

II Timothy 2:15

BAILEYISM #54

A sermonette makes a Christian-ette.

If you explain this to the others, you will be doing your duty as a worthy servant of Christ Jesus.

I Timothy 4:6

BAILEYISM #55

If you can earn salvation, you can *un*-earn salvation.

For it is by grace you have been saved, through faith—and this not from yourselves, it is the gift of God—not by works, so that no one can boast.

Ephesians 2:8-9

Salvation

BAILEYISM #56

Once you are saved, you are *always* saved!

I give them eternal life, and they shall never perish; no one can snatch them out of my hand.

John 10:28

Salvation

BAILEYISM #57

If you are able to sin and be comfortable, you'd better check out your salvation.

When people keep on sinning, it shows they belong to the devil.

I John 3:8

BAILEYISM #58

**It's one thing to be in Christ - that's salvation.
It's another thing for Christ to be in you - that's sanctification.**

Sanctify them by the truth; your word is truth.

John 17:17

BAILEYISM #59

Some people can know the Bible from cover to cover and still not know Jesus.

Not everyone who calls out to me, 'Lord! Lord!' will enter the Kingdom of Heaven.

Matthew 7:21

BAILEYISM #60

**If you keep doing
what you're doing,
you'll keep getting
what you're getting.**

*Let us stop going over the
basic teachings about
Christ again and again.
Let us go on instead and
become mature in our
understanding.*

Hebrews 6:1

When a person is born again he has two natures – and the one that wins is the one he feeds the most.

Live by the Spirit, and you will not gratify the desires of the sinful nature.

Galatians 5:16

BAILEYISM #62

God doesn't want to be a resident in your life; he wants to be President in your life.

Seek the Kingdom of God above all else, and live righteously, and he will give you everything you need.

Matthew 6:33

BAILEYISM #63

**Be a fat Christian -
faithful, available and
teachable.**

*But grow in the grace and
knowledge of our Lord
and Savior Jesus Christ.*

II Peter 3:18

Spiritual Growth

BAILEYISM #64

Christians should live in the world, but not of the world.

Do not conform any longer to the pattern of this world, but be transformed by the renewing of your mind.

Romans 12:2

Spiritual Growth

BAILEYISM #65

If you never face any resistance from the Devil, it's probably because the two of you are headed in the same direction.

So I say, walk by the spirit, and you will not gratify the desires of the flesh.

Galatians 5:16

BAILEYISM #66

Sometimes our affliction is our badge of identification with Jesus.

For it has been granted to you on behalf of Christ not only to believe on him, but also to suffer for him.

Philippians 1:29

Suffering

BAILEYISM #67

Experience is not always the best teacher, but it can be the most painful one.

The suffering you sent was good for me, for it taught me to pay attention to your principles.

Psalms 119:71

BAILEYISM #68

God will always give you inner strength to withstand the outer forces.

He gives strength to the weary and increases the power of the weak.

Isaiah 40:29

No one can escape the vicissitudes of life.

On earth you will have many trials and sorrows. But take heart, because I have overcome the world.

John 17:33

Christians are either entering a storm, in the middle of a storm, or coming out of a storm.

Consider it pure joy, my brothers, whenever you face trials of many kinds.

James 1:2

BAILEYISM #71

Unless your problem is bigger than a dead Jesus, God can handle your problem.

Is anything too hard for the Lord?

Genesis 18:14

BAILEYISM #72

If you think you're immune to suffering, keep living. Suffering will eventually knock on your door.

Everyone who wants to live a godly life in Christ Jesus will be persecuted.

II Timothy 3:12

BAILEYISM #73

It takes the spade of sorrow to dig the well of joy.

Those who sow in tears will reap with songs of joy.

Psalms 126:5

BAILEYISM #74

If you want to know how a person feels about God, take a look at his checkbook.

For where your treasure is, there your heart will be also.

Matthew 6:21

Tithes & Offerings

BAILEYISM #75

When God gives you a vision, he'll give you the provision.

And my God will meet all your needs according to his glorious riches in Christ Jesus.

Philippians 4:19

BAILEYISM #76

**God will send a
blessing to you so he
can send a blessing
through you.**

*It is more blessed to give
than to receive.*

Acts 20:35

Tithes & Offerings

BAILEYISM #77

Don't rob Peter to pay Paul.

How have we robbed you? In tithes and offerings.

Tithes & Offerings

BAILEYISM #78

If you're going on vacation, don't forget to leave God's money behind.

Honor the Lord with your wealth, with the first fruits of all your crops.

Proverbs 3:9

Tithes & Offerings

BAILEYISM #79

Patience is accepting a situation without giving God a deadline to remove it.

Don't be impatient for the Lord to act.

Psalms 37:34

Waiting

BAILEYISM #80

When you can't take life by the day, take it by the moment.

God is our refuge and strength, always ready to help in times of trouble.

Psalms 46:1

Waiting

**If you're worried about something you can change, it's foolishness;
if you're worried about something you cannot change, it's futile.**

Don't worry about anything. Instead pray about everything.

Philippians 4:6

BAILEYISM #82

Trust the heart of God when you can't trace the hand of God.

Trust in the Lord with all your heart
and lean not on your own understanding.

Proverbs 3:5

Worry

46151889R00051

Made in the USA
Middletown, DE
24 July 2017